SONGS
RECORDED BY

**NAT
KING
COLE**

VOLUME 5

MUSIC OF THE STARS
Rare Jazz and Popular Songs from The American Songbook

PROFESSIONAL MUSIC INSTITUTE

EXCLUSIVELY DISTRIBUTED BY

HAL•LEONARD®
CORPORATION

7777 W. BLUEMOUND RD. P.O. BOX 13819 MILWAUKEE, WI 53213

T0050718

Around The World

(From The Motion Picture "Around The World In 80 Days")

Lyric by Harold Adamson
Music by Victor Young

A -
-round the world I've searched for you, I trav - eled on, when hope was gone, to keep a ren - - dez - vous. I know some - where, some - time, some - how, You'd look at me, and I would see the smile you're smil - - - ing

All By Myself

Lyric and Music by
Irving Berlin

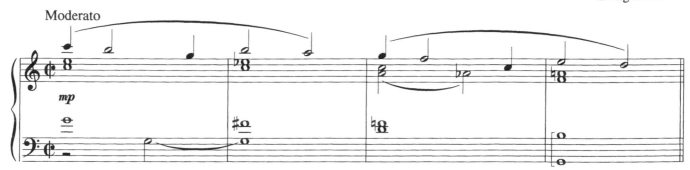

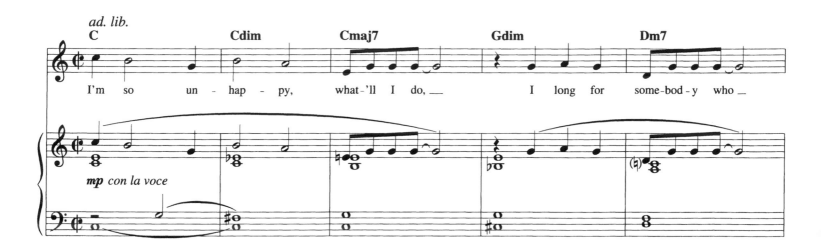

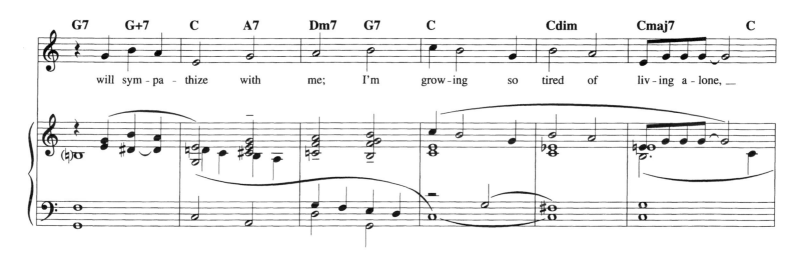

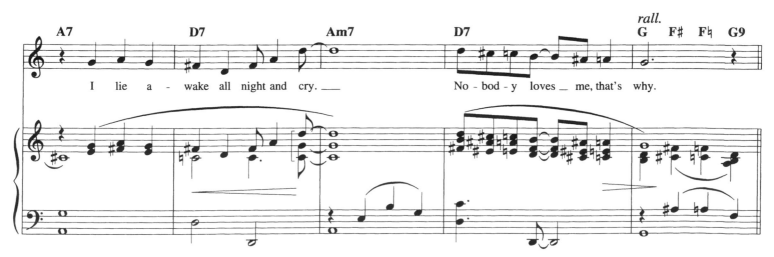

6

All by my-self ___ I get lone - ly, ___

Watch - ing the clock ___ on the shelf. ___ I'd love to

rest my wea - ry head on some - bod-y's shoul - der, ___ I hate ___ to grow

old - er, all by my - self. ___ - self. ___

All by myself 3-3

Avalon

Lyric by Al Jolson and Buddy DeSylva
Music by Vincent Rose

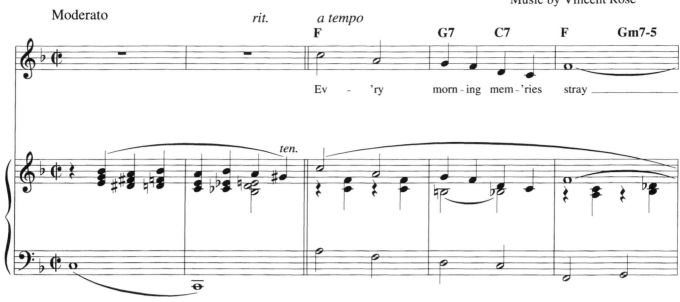

Ev - 'ry morn - ing mem - 'ries stray _____

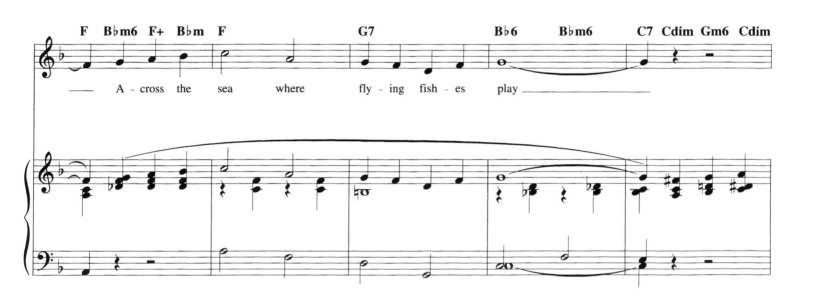

_____ A - cross the sea where fly - ing fish - es play _____

And as the night is fall – ing I find that I'm re - call – ing

8

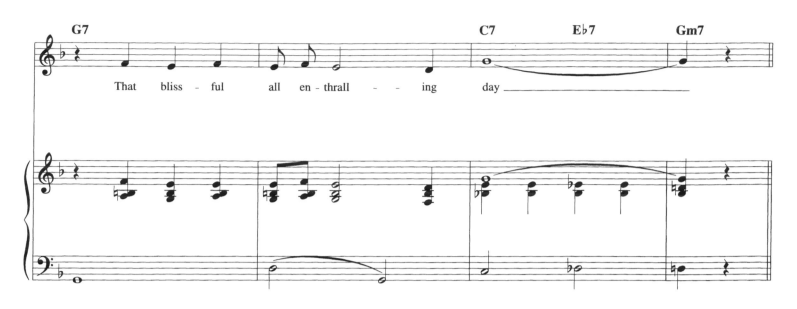

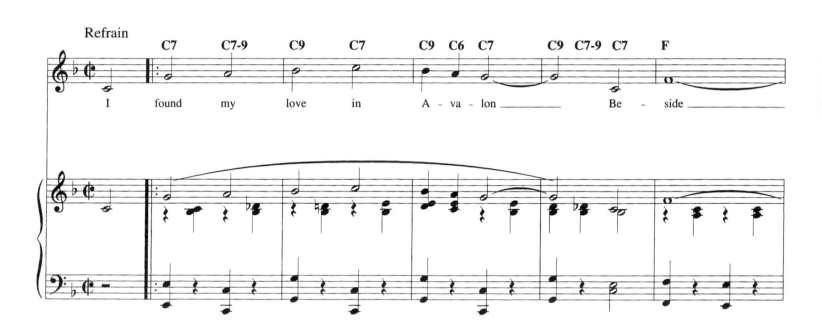

Avalon 2-3

Ballerina
(Dance Ballerina Dance)

Lyric by Bob Russell
Music by Carl Sigman

Crazy He Calls Me

Lyric by Bob Russell
Music by Carl Sigman

14

Blue Gardenia

Lyric and Music by
Bob Russell and Lester Lee

Destination Moon

Lyric by Roy Alfred
Music by Marvin Fisher

Medium bounce

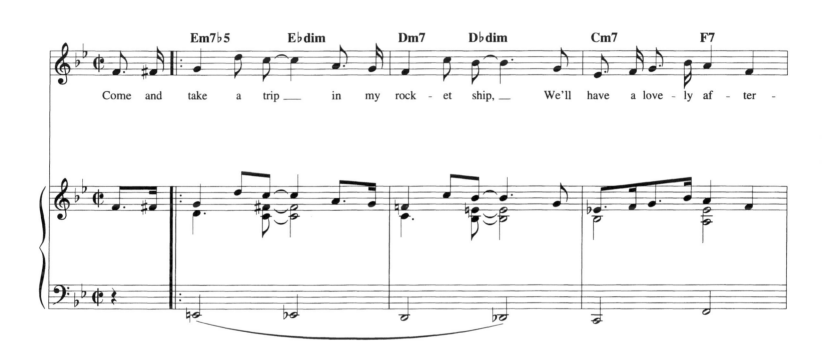

Come and take a trip __ in my rock - et ship, __ We'll have a love - ly af - ter -

- noon, __ Kiss the world good - bye and a - way we fly __ (Shhhh) __ des - ti - na - tion

Destination moon 2-3

20

Destination moon 3-3

Don't Get Around Much Anymore

Lyric by Bob Russell
Music by Duke Ellington

22

Don't get around much anymore 2-3

For All We Know

Lyric by Haven Gillespie
Music by J. Fred Coots

For all we know 2-3

26

It All Depends On You

Lyric and Music by
B. G. DeSylva, Lew Brown and Ray Henderson

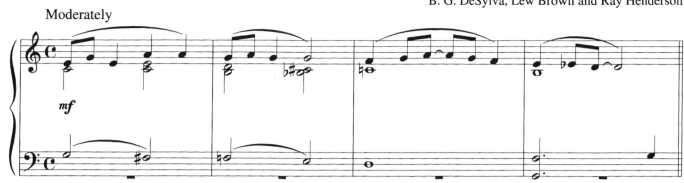

I can be lone - ly out in a crowd, I can be hum - ble, I can be proud, It

All De - pends On You. _____

I can save mon - ey or spend it, go right on liv - ing or end it.

There Goes My Heart

Lyric by Benny Davis
Music by Abner Silver

It's All In The Game

Lyric by Carl Sigman
Music by Charles G. Dawes

34

It's all in the game 3-3

The Late, Late Show

Lyric by Roy Alfred
Music by Murray Berlin

Gee! It's co-sy in the park to-night, _ When you cud-dle up and hold me tight; _

Stars a-bove, _ they seem, _ to know, _ We're put-ting on the late, late show. _

The late, late show 3-3

My Sugar Is So Refined

Lyric by Sylvia Dee
Music by Sidney Lippman

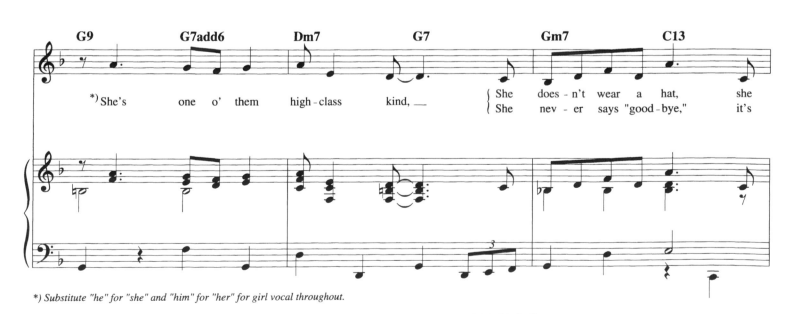

*) Substitute "he" for "she" and "him" for "her" for girl vocal throughout.

My sugar is so refined 2-4

Sentimantal Journey

Lyric and Music by
Bud Green, Les Brown and Ben Homer

Very slow

Gon - na take a sen - ti - men - tal jour - ney, Gon - na set my

heart at ease, ___ Gon - na make a sen - ti - men - tal jour - ney

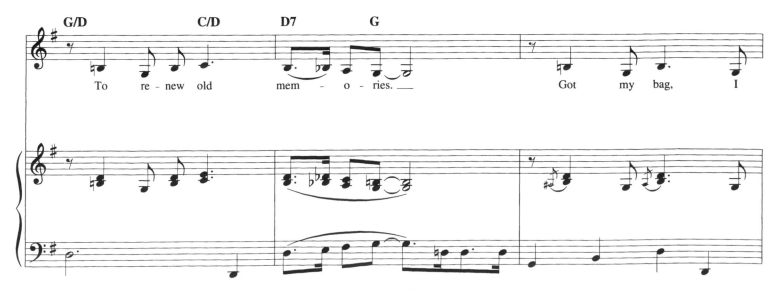

To re - new old mem - o - ries. ___ Got my bag, I

Teach Me Tonight

Lyric by Sammy Cahn
Music by Gene DePaul

Did you say, "I've got a lot to learn?" _____ Well, don't think I'm try-ing not to learn. Since this is the per-fect spot to learn, teach me to - night. Start-ing with the "A, B,

46

Teach me tonight 2-3

Teach me tonight 3-3

There Will Never Be Another You

Lyric by Mack Gordon
Music by Harry Warren

50

There will never be another you 3-3

Lyric and Music by
Henry Nemo

Too Young

Lyric by Sylvia Dee
Music by Sidney Lippman

They try to tell us we're TOO YOUNG

TOO YOUNG to real-ly be in love.

They say that love's a word, a word we're on-ly

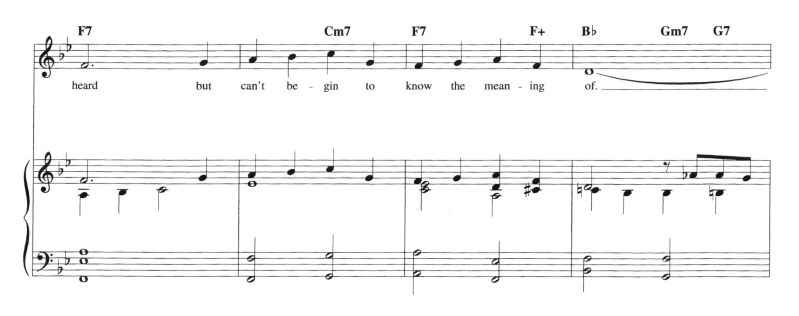

heard but can't be - gin to know the mean - ing of. ____

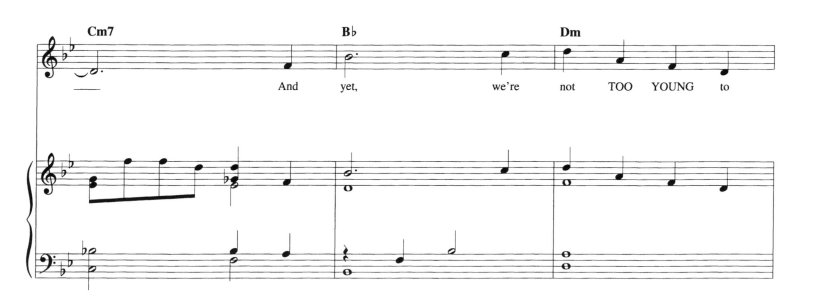

____ And yet, we're not TOO YOUNG to

know ____ this love will last tho' years may

Too young 2-3

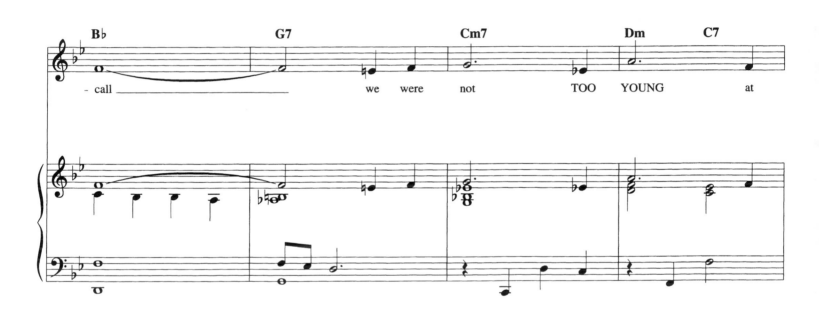

Two Different Worlds

Lyric by Sid Wayne
Music by Al Frisch

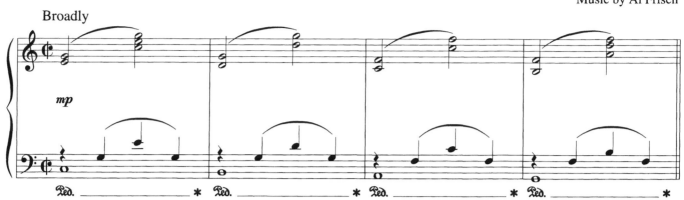

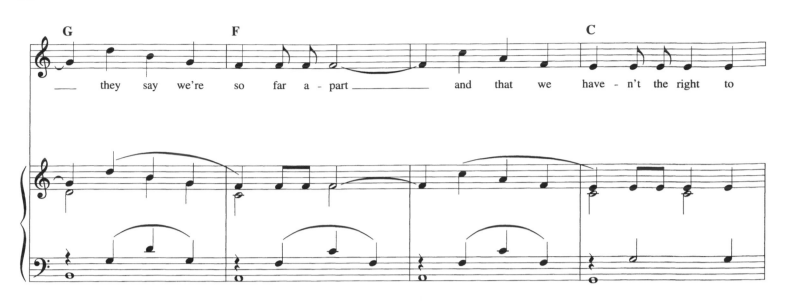

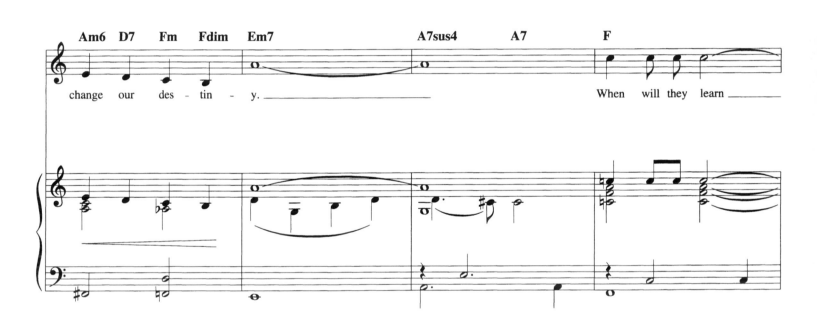

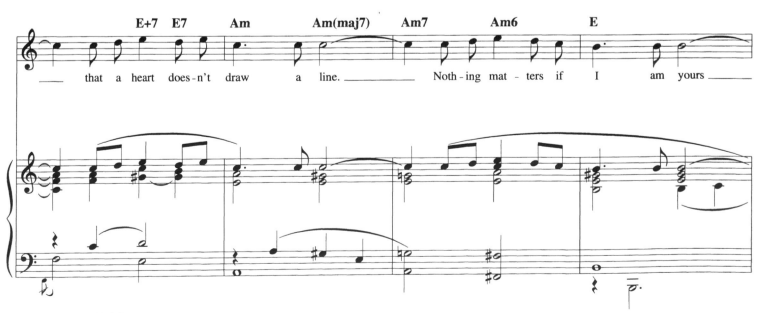

Two different worlds 2-3

Two different worlds 3-3

You Go To My Head

Lyric by Haven Gillespie
Music by J. Fred Coots

You go to my head __ and you lin-ger like a

haunt-ing re - frain, __ and I find you spin-ning 'round in my brain __

like the bub-bles in a glass of cham - pagne. __ You

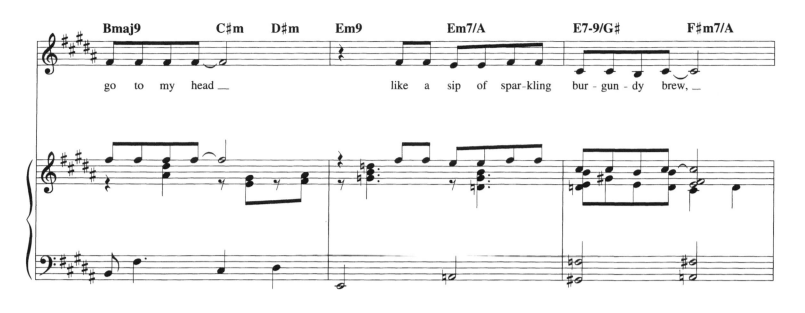

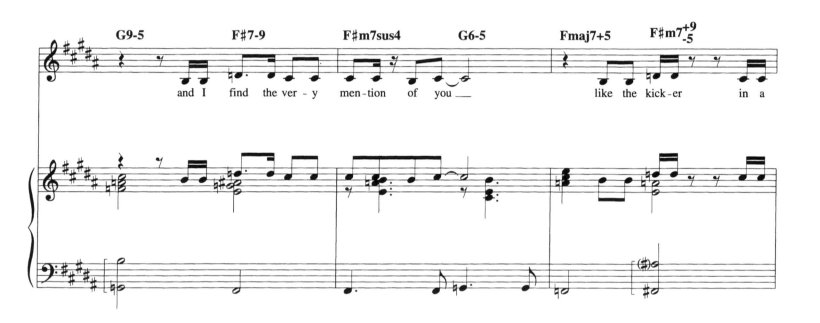

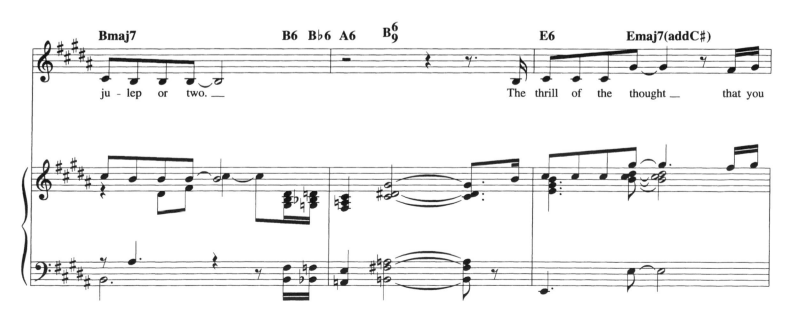

62

You go to my head 3-4

Selected Discography

The many classic songs in this book have been recorded by hundreds of great performers in many different styles over the years. Listed below are just a few of the favorite CD Recordings chosen by our staff for you to consider. In most cases we have tried to list the original album title, however all of them appear on reissue compilations as well.

All By Myself
Nat "King" Cole "Unforgettable Collection"
Ella Fitzgerald "The Irving Berlin Songbook"
Bobby Darin "Spotlight on Bobby Darin"

Around The World
Nat "King" Cole "Unforgettable Collection"
Matt Monro "Very Best of Matt Monro"
Frank Sinatra "Come Fly With Me"

Avalon
Nat "King" Cole "The Collection Box Set"
Anita O'Day "The Diva Series"
Natalie Cole "Unforgettable With Love"

Ballerina (Dance, Ballerina, Dance)
Nat "King" Cole "Classic Singles"
Mel Torme "Love Me Or Leave Me"
Sammy Davis Jr. "The Nat "King" Cole Songbook"

Blue Gardenia
Nat "King" Cole "The Nat "King" Cole Story"
Dinah Washington "Dinah's Finest Hour"
Mark Murphy "Sings Nat "King" Cole"

Crazy She Calls Me
Nat "King" Cole "Spotlight on Nat "King" Cole"
Tony Bennett "On Holiday"
Rod Stewart "Great American Songbook Vol. # 2

Destination Moon
Nat "King" Cole "The Greatest Hits"
Dinah Washington "Best of Dinah Washington"
J Street Jumpers "Good For Stomping"

Don't Get Around Much Anymore
Nat "King" Cole "The Billy May Sessions"
Mose Allison "Greatest Hits"
Tony Bennett "The Very Thought of You"

For All We Know
Nat "King" Cole "Love Songs"
Crystal Gayle "All My Tomorrows"
Chet Baker "Chet Baker Sings"

It All Depends On You
Nat "King" Cole "Wonderful Music of Nat "King" Cole"
Steve Tyrell "Standard Time"
Frank Sinatra "Swingin' Sessions"

It's All In The Game
Nat "King" Cole "Love Is The Thing"
Art Garfunkel "Up 'Til Now"
George Benson "Weekend In LA"

The Late, Late Show
Nat "King" Cole "Collector's Edition"
Dakota Staton "Spotlight on Dakota Staton"
Janis Siegal "I Wish You Love"

My Sugar Is So Refined
Nat "King" Cole "Live At The Circle Room"
Peggy Lee "Complete Capitol Transcriptions"
Johnny Mercer "Capitol Collectors Series"

Sentimental Journey
Tony Bennett "Here's To The Ladies"
Renee Olstead "Renee Olstead"
Frank Sinatra "Come Swing With Me"

Teach Me Tonight"
Nat "King" Cole "The King Swings"
Nancy Wilson "Something Wonderful"
Joe Williams "Joe Williams' Finest Hour"

There Goes My Heart
Nat "King" Cole "Let's Fall In Love"
Etta Jones "From The Heart"
Johnny Hartman "Just You, Just Me"

There Will Never Be Another You
Nat "King" Cole "A Portrait of Nat "King" Cole
Julie London "The Best of Julie London"
Frank Sinatra "Point of No Return"

'Tis Autumn
Nat "King" Cole "Cool Cole"
Stacey Kent "The Boy Next Door"
Mark Murphy "Complete Nat "King" Cole Songbook"

Too Young
Nat "King" Cole "Let's Fall In Love"
Englebert Humperdinck "You Belong To My Heart"
Natalie Cole "Unforgettable With Love"

Two Different Worlds
Nat "King" Cole "Essentials"
La Verne Butler "Daydreamin'"
Englebert Humperdinck "This Is My Life"

You Go To My Head
Tony Bennett "Perfectly Frank"
Ann Hampton Callaway "Bring Back Romance"
Bobby Caldwell "Blue Condition"